# GOD HUNGER

# GOD HUNGER
## DISCOVERING THE MYSTIC IN ALL OF US

John Kirvan

SORIN BOOKS
Notre Dame, IN

John Kirvan is the author of the highly successful *Thirty Days with a Great Spiritual Teacher* series, a library of fourteen books which offer the wisdom of the mystics for daily meditation. He currently lives in Southern California where he writes primarily about classical spirituality.

International Standard Book Number: 1-893732-03-7

Library of Congress Catalog Card Number: 99-62069

Cover design by: Angela Moody

Cover photo by: Tony Stone Images, Inc.

Text design by Katherine Robinson Coleman

Printed and bound in the United States of America

For F. B.

And with gratitude to all of those whose love, friendship, and support over these last years have made it possible for me to be who I am and to do what it is that I do. With special thanks to those who read these pages in their early stages and encouraged me to "get on with it."

# Contents

# PART ONE

# God Hunger

This hunger is better than any other fullness;
this poverty better than all other wealth.

—C. S. LEWIS

For the first time in our adult lives many of us are freely admitting to an aching spiritual emptiness, the full depth of which we are only gradually becoming aware.

The good news is that it is now possible to make this admission without being considered a religious nut—or a psychotic.

The bad news is that "spirituality" is in danger of becoming a meaningless word used to describe anything that can't be tied down, a synonym for warm-fuzziness.

The world-class model hyping her book of beauty hints on TV reduces spirituality to "the big beauty tip of the decade." Others diminish spirituality to the instant, unquestioning acceptance of a pet, the after-glow of a tennis tournament, or the interior decor of a blues club.

We are offered pop psychology, greeting-card wisdom, and gift-book comfort. They are not enough to satisfy the wrenching spiritual hunger that many of us are feeling. "The very best" is no longer good enough. From experience we know we need more than the "fix" of a self-help book, or even the rewards of the most responsible therapy. We know that the spiritual lives we seek go far beyond and deeper than being well adjusted. We know, too, that the spirituality for which we hunger is not the same as a renewed morality, that it goes beyond a life of good behavior, kind deeds and motivations. It goes beyond an archeological dig into childhood religion. We need more than talk of "soul" that reduces our spirits to a measure of energy.

We are more than a little weary of spiritual junk food.

We are beginning to realize that we hunger for God and that for far too long we have settled for far too little. This basic, primal hunger for God may be the least recognized and acknowledged aspect of today's highly publicized spiritual quest and our own personal journeys.

We want what the great mystics sought and found—not an occasional comforting word but a perspective-shattering glimpse of God, not one more promise of bliss in ten days and ten steps but a here-and-now taste of eternity. Nothing less will satisfy this hunger, too long denied.

There, we've said it. We have used the word *mystic*. And if it is true that the word *spirituality* has been drugged into meaninglessness by overuse and careless use, it is even more true that the word mystic is avoided, consigned to our too-embarrassing-to-use vocabulary. There is, we are inclined to think, something pretentious, precious, even preposterous about applying that word to the desires we feel so deeply in our hearts and souls.

This is not new. A little over fifty years ago, E. Allison Peers, the translator and biographer of John of the Cross and Teresa of Avila, noted that the word *mystic* had for some time "been getting into the wrong company."

For one thing, mysticism is consistently and confusedly identified with the highly publicized, easily dramatized special effects of the spiritual life—rare, exotic phenomena such as levitation and stigmata that mark the lives of some who have sought to live with God. But these effects are not the reward for spiritual success, signs of God's approval, any more than their lack is a mark of spiritual failure, a sign of God's indifference.

"A mystic," Peers wrote, "is a person who has fallen in love with God. We are not afraid of lovers—no indeed: 'all the world loves a lover.' They attract us by their ardor, their single-mindedness, their yearning to be one with the object of their love." Mysticism is nothing more or less than a love-driven way of knowing God that is centered in direct, immediate experience of God's presence—or absence—as contrasted with the efforts of our minds to think through, capture, and describe the object of our belief in clear language, theological subtlety, or scientific precision. And it is a way of living that makes this consciousness of God's presence the shaping context, the compelling energy of our lives. "To the questing soul no mere message from God suffices. She cries out for God himself."

Nevertheless it is hard to describe our own spiritual yearning, our divine dreaming, our stuttering prayers as mystical, because we are so ordinary. It is far more embarrassing than we care to admit. Even if we are unaware of the centuries-long debate about mysticism (whether, that is, it is a rare calling or one that is a grace extended to every believer), we find ourselves presuming and living as though the call to live in the presence of God is not for such as we. Not everyone will understand. For while it has become okay to speak in vague spiritual generalities, even of angels and miracles, in the most unbelieving of situations, it is still considered eccentric, strange, and even embarrassing to admit to our hunger for God, even our tentative interest. We are afraid, perhaps, that what we feel deep in the silence of our souls is too fragile for the light of day, too personal for public exposure. We are tongue-tied, even at times ashamed.

And it is not just that we shy from public confession; it is that we hardly dare to speak the word in the silence of our own souls. If it is true, as all the mystics have said, that ultimately we find God within, what makes us think that God would be at home within us? Others, perhaps. In us? Hardly!

But the hunger of our souls settles the debate, forces us to face our fears and our hesitancies. We want contact with God. If it is within that we shall find God, and if this be mysticism, so be it.

We must also admit that we are often embarrassed and fearful of the company in which we could find ourselves. Men and women justify killing with the announcement that they have heard God's voice and are being obedient to God's commands. The history of every people seems blood-soaked in the intolerance of believers, in their hatred for those who differ, in their discrimination against those who do not believe or behave as they do. See today's paper, whatever day this is. God forbid that we should be associated with these.

Still another fear holds us back—the fear, after a lifetime of seeking recognition as achievers, of being thought losers in a world that treasures only its winners, fear of being looked down upon as those who having lost the battle with this world retreat whimpering into the next.

But we know that it is God we want, that we want so hungrily but seek so timidly. Not the God of the headlines that shrinks our souls, not the God that paralyzes us in fear, or the God who is called upon to justify hatred and cruelty. We seek, rather, the God of the mystics who alone can make of us all that we are meant to be. We seek the God who can expand our souls to the point of bursting, the God whose gift of freedom shatters our every expectation, the God who is love writ so large that we will never exhaust its promises.

The God we seek is not the first cause, the last temptation, the chilly abstraction of the best our minds can do, but the subject and object of a passion that overwhelms us even as it releases the very heart of our fallible and finite humanity.

This does not mean that we are seeking to be monks, theologians, evangelists, or even church-goers. We are not seeking, as one author puts it, "religiosity lived for its own sake."

But we are seeking to overthrow many of the values by which we have measured our humanity and sought our fulfillment and that in the end have left us empty and hungry for something more. We are seeking to replace "success" as the standard of our lives with a spirit-centeredness in which what we cannot see will replace in importance what we have always seen and relied on. It's a reversal that requires us to turn our lives upside down, inside out.

Scary? Yes. Feeding our spiritual hunger demands more of us than a warm, effortless embrace of serenity. This is no journey for the timid but a way marked, if we are wise, by a profound fear of what meeting God might be like. It is, says scripture, a terrible thing to fall into the hands of the living God. The great work of Jewish mysticism, the Kabbalah, has been traditionally forbidden to any but the most stable, the most mature, those who have the benefit of age. Why? Because the pursuit of God is a dangerous passage through treacherous waters that at every turn threaten to drown all but the most seasoned spiritual travelers. God does invite us on the journey, but it is for spiritual risk-takers.

But an impossible journey? No. We are not the first to travel this path, we are not without guidance, and we are not alone.

The mystical quest for God takes us along well-traveled paths, blazed over the centuries by men and women of every religious and spiritual tradition who have accepted nothing less than dwelling consciously in the presence of God as the heart of their lives, the object of their human journey—and ours.

Hundreds of them have left records of their day-to-day experiences along the way, recording what they learned so as to make our journey if not easier, at least less treacherous. Their lives and words are there to be drawn from at every point in our quest for God. "This," they say, each in their own way, "is what it is like to meet God. These are the blessings. These are the terrors."

The lives and words of these men and women give us reason to hope, and perhaps even more important, permission to hope.

It is a hope with roots in the visions of Ezekiel, nearly 600 years before the Christian era. It includes desert hermits of the fifteenth century and social activists of the twentieth. Some of them, like Francis of Assisi, are household names; others, like Evagrius Ponticus, are barely known even to scholars of the spiritual life. In the west it includes Jews and Moslems and Christians whose amazing unanimity demonstrates that the pursuit of a spiritual life is not confined to one place or time, to one lifestyle, to a single race, nationality, gender, temperament, or religious tradition. Some, like Ezekiel and Paul, have left their stories in scripture. Others, like Augustine and Rumi, have created classic works of literature. The words of others would have been lost to us had they not been recorded by followers. Some are anonymous, gathered by followers into works such as the Kabbalah. "The spirit breathes where it will."

Even in us.

In these pages you will find mystics of the Jewish scriptures cheek by jowl with twentieth-century Christians and a Sufi poet by the side of an eastern Christian, a gathering that reminds us that not only is there nothing new in the tradition but that its very consistency is a source of strength and reassurance.

The same range of great spiritual experiences and themes dominates all their lives and traditions. Foremost is the practice of the presence of God. It is a theme that stresses the accessibility of God, the ongoing concern, the extraordinary sense of familiarity that some traditions would find offensive but which is the very air that western mystics breathe. This same tradition, in the very same instance, stresses that the God with whom we share the air is finally a total mystery, beyond our knowing, who escapes our every attempt to confine and define God's being. This God is found as often, if not more often, in darkness as in light, in that frightening world where all our words and worlds end.

Paradox is in fact a hallmark of western spirituality, an ongoing reminder that mystery is the heart, the atmosphere and completion of our spiritual quest, that the ultimately untouchable is forever at our fingertips.

The world is where we experience God, but the world in the end is never enough—a friend at any given moment, our seducer at the next. Solitude and silence may be the meat and potatoes of our prayer lives, but they are empty of nourishment when separated from service of our brothers and sisters. And so it goes, running through their lives and words, tantalizing, enveloping mystery and present, insistent actuality.

We need also to remember that one of the most profound themes of western spirituality is that the God we pursue is also our pursuer, that what keeps us apart is not God's distance but our flight, that we need, perhaps more than anything else, to stop running and let ourselves be caught.

For if there is a human hunger for God, it is matched by God's hunger for union with us, a hunger that extends not just to a few spiritually talented souls but to all of us, not just to the best of us but to the least of us.

We need, therefore, to be bold. Nothing is a greater obstacle to a spiritual life than a false modesty, the notion that we are too unimportant to be a subject of God's greatest gifts, the object of God's unwavering desire. Believe Teresa of Avila when she says: "We do not have to be bashful with God."

We are invited to join the company of God seekers. Our attention is requested by the Hound of Heaven.

It is time to stop running.

# PART TWO

# God Seeking: 50 Experiences for the Soul

Moses' vision of God began with light.
Afterwards God spoke to him in a cloud.
But when Moses rose higher
and became more perfect,
he saw God in the darkness.

—GREGORY OF NYSSA

In the end, searching for God is not a journey of the mind but of the soul. Ideas surrender to wonder. Words are a pathway into silence. And light ends in the darkness of a God who escapes our every effort at definition.

The pages that follow, therefore, are not for reading but for praying, for unwrapping the mystery, pulling back one veil at a time, knowing with each hope-filled, tentative gesture that the veils are without number, the mystery beyond plumbing.

In these pages you are being invited to explore ten basic elements of classical western spirituality by exploring the lives and writings of ten of the great spiritual teachers and by exploring your own soul and its journey.

The exploration, if it is to lead anywhere, must be conducted prayerfully, that is, with your heart open, from that place within all of us that Dag Hammarskjöld calls "a center of stillness surrounded by silence." What you seek on your journey is not a solution to a problem, not the answer to a question, but an encounter with mystery that will by very definition far exceed the best efforts of your mind, the uttermost limits of your imagination.

You are not asked to abandon your intelligence or surrender your sanity but to rely on the tools of the spirit, several of which are employed in the exploration of each theme.

Each section is introduced with an "epigram," a meditation-provoking passage taken from the writings of the teacher with whom you will explore it. You are invited to stop and pray it through. A short reading then develops the epigram and introduces the life and times of the teacher, the world in which he or she experienced God, and the unique characteristics of his or her experience.

Then come five experiences for the soul, each designed to involve you in the three great classic prayer forms of western spirituality.

There are "mantras," short, pithy, often epigrammatic sentences that by way of paradox and irony catch the essence of a great spiritual truth. They are easily committed to memory and often make their impact by constant repetition.

There are short spiritual readings—meditations. It is a form of prayer that best allows us to summon up silence, to focus our wildly work-family-news-distracted souls.

And finally there are short intercessory prayers in which we speak directly to the God whose presence we celebrate. Some would say that this is the most revealing of all our prayers, for in this moment we speak to the God in whom we truly believe, the one we address, as someone has said, when nobody else is listening. You may use the words provided, but your own will be more revealing, more searching.

How do you use these exercises? Any way you want. On any schedule, at any interval that is convenient, comfortable, or rewarding. Do the meditation in the morning, if you prefer, and the prayer at night. Or do the whole thing in one snatched period of quiet. Do what you want. But do exercise an element of regularity. Without it you could miss out because of mere forgetfulness or laziness.

The themes follow the pattern experienced by Moses and described in the epigram by Gregory of

Nyssa that opens this section of the book. They move from light through clouds to darkness—that darkness at the mountaintop on which Moses saw God. It is a passage that is true of every spiritual quest.

But you must not forget as you explore the experience of those who have gone before, as you exercise your own soul in this pursuit of mystery, that your personal quest for God is at its depth a unique moment in history. Millions have preceded you. But this is the first time you and God have met. There has never been anyone quite like you. There has never been a spiritual moment quite like this.

One of the great theologians of this century, Karl Rahner, puts it this way: "Each individual man or woman is a unique and unrepeatable term of God's creative love. Each must find their path to God in a way that is proper to themselves."

You will if you faithfully follow the same path followed by Moses—a journey from light through clouds to darkness.

Be prepared, in any case, to be surprised, because no one is more surprising than God. You may in the end, as the Kabbalah says, despite your most careful planning and the most demanding discipline, "stumble" onto God. "Whoever delves into mysticism cannot help but stumble, as it is written: 'This stumbling block is our hand. We cannot grasp these things unless we stumble over them.'"

# Longing

C. S. LEWIS

Our lifelong nostalgia,
our longing to be reunited
with something in the universe
from which we feel cut off,
to be on the inside of some door
which we have always seen from the outside,
is no mere neurotic fantasy,
but the truest index of our situation.

—C. S. LEWIS

# Longing

*Longing* is such a commonplace word with such connotations of adolescent romanticism that at first it is not only hard to accept it as a key to spirituality, it is almost embarrassing.

But it belongs in the vocabulary of the soul because we live, as C. S. Lewis reminds us, with a "lifelong nostalgia . . . a longing to be reunited with something in the universe from which we feel cut off." It is that "old ache" that will not go away.

But it's not meant to go away. It's meant to be lifelong. It must be lifelong, because its object will forever exceed our grasp. The emptiness, the hunger at its core is too great to be filled with anything but a God who exceeds our every attempt at comprehension.

If it does go away it means that we have found a substitute for God.

It is a hard notion for those of us who have spent our lives pinning down every dream, believing that joy comes only with possession, to grasp that longing is an end in itself, that the best thing we can possess is a longing for what we may never have.

Our joy is in the sheer act of hoping, of longing for what is behind the door at which our hearts so constantly knock.

It is better to long and never possess than not to have longed at all, never to have ached for what lies beyond our reach. This is something that C. S. Lewis knew well.

# C. S. Lewis
## (1898-1963)

Not every spiritual master makes it to Hollywood as the hero of a great love story—Shadowlands. Then again not every spiritual master has used network radio to introduce some of the most important spiritual masterpieces of his or her age.

But if these facts make C. S. Lewis different and intriguing in a spiritual tradition that too often is uncomfortable with marriage and fame, they are not what make him important.

What makes him important is that despite a lifetime as a university don with a decidedly conservative point of view, his insights are so grounded in common sense, so enriched with imagination, clarity, and wit, that his appeal breaks down denominational barriers. He takes seriously feelings we know well but that an age of psychoanalysis too often dismisses as immaturity.

We read his words and recognize ourselves. They ring true, their spiritual demands reasonable, even when they upset our expectations and carry us far beyond our comfort zone.

His attitude toward "longing" is typical. There is a sweetness about the word, a softness. But no sooner has Lewis spoken it than we find ourselves plummeting into a spiritual world as profound as any that John of the Cross might have described.

There comes a moment when we are tempted to draw back. "Supposing we really found what we were longing for. We never meant it to come to that! Worse still, supposing He had found us?"

The comfortable read, the familiar word, becomes the demanding encounter. The comfortable life opens into a world for which our hearts may ache but which holds the terror of the unexpected and the unknown. But we know that with Lewis, we are in good hands.

There is something reassuring about a spiritual master who has been surprised by the joy of an unexpected love and been shattered by her painful passing. We can trust such a teacher, even as we share his longing.

# I

---

What does not satisfy when we find it,
was not the thing we were desiring.

—C. S. LEWIS

"Your eyes," our mothers told us, "are bigger than your stomach."

What we have yet to learn is that our eyes are never big enough for our souls. We dream too small. We are forever chasing after a thousand things that masquerade as the desire of our souls—as God; so many sirens calling us, if not to destruction, at least to distraction and frustration.

We need to look them in the face and say: "No, you are not it. You are not what I desire. . . . You are not what I long for.

"You, whoever you are, whatever you are, are not enough.

"I'm looking for God."

## LET US PRAY

Stir in my soul
dreams as big as the love you offer,
for even the impossible dream
is too small
for those you have created in your image.
Let me see through the impostors
that knock forever at the door of my soul,
promising what only you can give.
Replace my small dreams
with your invitation.

# 2

This hunger is better than any other fullness;
this poverty better than all other wealth.

—C. S. LEWIS

God comes to us not as food but as hunger, not as
presence but as distance felt, not as fulfillment but as
longing, not as love consummated but as desire
enkindled.

God does not take away our loneliness but intensifies
it.

God does not answer our questions but floods our
souls with ever-expanding mystery.

God does not soothe that "old ache" but deepens it.

God does not open the door but prompts us to go on
knocking.

For our hunger is a joyful longing.

Our hunger is God made present.

## LET US PRAY

Do not take away the hunger of my soul
or let me fill it with spiritual trifles,
ready to hand,
sweet to the taste,
but good for only a moment's satisfaction.

Deepen my hunger.
Enkindle my desire.
Come to me
in the longing in my heart,
for in my emptiness
you are present.

# 3

God gives his gifts
where he finds the vessel empty enough
to receive them.

—C. S. LEWIS

Nothing is more receptive to the gifts of God than that special emptiness that is longing.

The temptation, however, is to come to God bearing gifts, proofs, as it were, that we are worthy of his generosity. We have been taught, after all, to exchange gifts, to return favors, to keep generosity in balance.

But God "gives," says St. Augustine, "where he finds empty hands."

"A man whose hands are full of parcels," adds Lewis, "cannot receive a gift."

Only the uncluttered emptiness of outstretched hands, our unashamed longing leaves room for God.

## LET US PRAY

I have been taught
to prove my worthiness,
so it is not easy
to come before you
with empty hands.
But your love is not earned.
Help me then
to empty my cluttered heart,
and out of its newfound emptiness
let me reach out
to where your generosity awaits.

# 4

Our whole being by its very nature
is one vast need
incomplete, preparatory, empty yet cluttered.

—C. S. LEWIS

There are other names for that "old ache"—none of them flattering, none of them easily embraced by those of us who measure our lives by standards of achievement and control.

We are "one vast need."

The measure of our spirit is not fulfillment but emptiness. We are the incomplete.

We can ignore our neediness, paper over it, or try to hide from it in the clutter of our lives.

Or we can accept our emptiness for what it is: the joyful root and measure of our longing.

## LET US PRAY

I am one of the empty ones,
one of the incomplete ones,
the needy,
the dissatisfied.
I hide from you
in the clutter of my heart
papering over my neediness
with words.
Let me accept my emptiness
for what it is:
the joyful root
and measure of my longing.

# 5

If God does not show himself,
nothing we can do will enable us to find him.

—C. S. LEWIS

We long to catch a glimpse of God.

In this and this alone is the joy of our longing, and its value. For as long as we center our longing in anything short of God, or even in what the world tells us is beyond God, it is impossible for God to show himself to us.

Beyond longing, beyond openness and readiness, there is nothing we can do to insure our finding God. "When we come to knowing God," Lewis reminds us, "the initiative lies on his side."

But when it comes to blocking God's approach and clouding our sight, the initiative is ours. In this only are we the masters of our souls, the doorkeepers of longing.

To desire what is on the other side of the door, to open it, to leave it open, is not to feed some neurotic fantasy but to recognize "the truest index of our situation."

## LET US PRAY

The most I can do
is to open my heart
and leave it open,
so that you can show yourself.
It is your turn.
As it always is.
As for me,
let me stand clear.
Let me get out of your way.

# Looking

## THOMAS MERTON

This is the land
where you have given me
roots in eternity,
O God of heaven and earth.
This is the burning, promised land,
the house of God,
the gate of heaven,
the place of peace,
the place of silence. . . .

—THOMAS MERTON

# Locating God

The temptation, of course, is to look in all the old familiar places for all of God's familiar faces.

We turn quickly and with warm easiness to the towering majesty of a mountain, to the insistent, uninterrupted power of the sea, to the sun-blotched quiet darkness of a forest, to the enveloping serenity of an isolated beach. On another day we recognize God in the sudden, indiscriminate violence of a storm, the uprooting destruction of a shaken earth, or the terrible fury of seas that swallow lives.

We find it easy and convenient—"heart-warming"—to trace the features of God in small miracles, in the face of a newborn child, in the lined wisdom of an aging life, in sudden, unexpected moments of generosity and care, in love of and for another. We also recognize God's face, less kindly, less gently, in sudden death, in lingering pain, in loss, and in failure.

The problem with this is that we pre-define God. We impose limits on God we would never impose on our friends, deciding a lifetime in advance what kind of God shall enter our lives and under what conditions, a program that in everyday relationships would leave us friendless or lifeless. Our choice may not be so crude as that between a fire-hurling bearded old man and a soft-faced bare-foot youth. But we prefer that there be no surprises, no shattering of our preconceptions. We confine our search to suitable places. And we find only the God of our limited expectations.

If, moreover, we confine our spiritual search to wherever the beauty, the power, and the terror of our world and our lives leaves us overwhelmed and breathless with wonder and fear we may miss the revelation of God that awaits us around the next corner, in the dusty crannies of our unexplored lives, wherever we could be caught by surprise.

"I am," says God, "where you are. No place is a stranger to my presence, no time of day, no time of your life. I am with you all days even to the end of time."

Be open. We are already and always in the presence of the God we seek, and God is present in us. This is the promised land. There is no other.

No one has known this better than Thomas Merton, the twentieth-century monk who sought God not only in the vowed silence of monastic life but in the anguish of history.

# Thomas Merton
## (1915-1968)

Thomas Merton was by vow committed to silence and hiddenness within the walls of a Trappist monastery in Kentucky. But he became one the most frequently heard and heeded spiritual voices of our twentieth century because he was committed by faith to the proposition that we cannot find God "by barricading ourselves inside our own souls."

From the moment in 1948 when his autobiography, *The Seven Storey Mountain*, erupted from his monastic cell to top the bestseller lists to his accidental death in Bangkok twenty years later, he produced a flood of books, articles, and letters that crossed denominational and traditional boundaries, made the contemplative life "thinkable" in an activist secular culture, and erased the line isolating contemplative prayer from social concern.

He would not allow monastery walls to make him "a guilty bystander" to the events that shaped his times and the lives of millions, a co-conspirator by silence to the sins of the nations. Despite his choice to live as a hermit on the grounds of his monastery, his voice, born in silence, became one of the clearest and most influential heard in the cacophonous days of the Vietnam War.

Thomas Merton was a monk who recognized that the discovery and love of God could not be confined to any one time or place—not to his cell, not to the monastery fields, not even to his own religious tradition.

"Doping our minds and isolating ourselves from everything that lives," he told his readers, "merely deadens us to all the opportunities for love."

The spiritual life, he wrote, is a continual discovery of God in new and unexpected places. And "these discoveries are sometimes most profitable when we find him in something we had tended to overlook and even despise. Then the awakening is purer and its effect more keen, because he was so close at hand and we neglected him."

This land where we find ourselves is the "burning promised land." This is "the house of God."

This is the place. This is the time. There is no other.

# I

His truth and his love pervade all things as the light and heat of the sun.

—THOMAS MERTON

Dramatic moments come and go. We return from the sea to the city. We leave the forest for the streets. We exchange serenity for the confusion of our homes, classrooms, and workplaces. Wonder and awe, joy and pain give way to exasperation and frustration. Clouds obscure the sun. The baby cries. The old man complains. The traffic snarls. The quiet, prayerful end of the day gives way to morning. Sunday passes. Monday dawns.

Our lives go on. So if we are to find God it will have to be where we are at any given moment—not just in the bright, glowing times and places when the world is a very special place or in the worst of times when he seems our only and last refuge, but in the ordinary, confining, demanding, and rarely dramatic days of our lives.

## LET US PRAY

Lord, unless I am able to trust the ordinary,
the commonplaces of my life,
I will surely miss
your all-enveloping presence.
You are where I am at every moment,
at this very moment.
Let me breathe in your presence and feel your warmth
wherever I am,
whatever I am doing.

# 2

The only One who can teach me to find God, is God, himself, alone.

—THOMAS MERTON

We act sometimes as though we could teach ourselves, knowing in advance where and when and how God will make his presence known to us.

We profess that we believe God to be everywhere, but we act sometimes as though we really think that God is to be found primarily, if not exclusively, at times and places that are specifically marked "Sacred . . . God present here!"

But God is not bound by our limitations. He is not restricted to the Sabbath's dawn, to 11 a.m. on Sundays and 8 p.m. on Wednesdays, or to the buildings we have set aside for God. God is where we are. And where we are not. All the time. No exceptions.

We can expect to be surprised by God.

## LET US PRAY

Lord, I am a slow learner.
As often as I am told
that you will make your presence known
where and when you please,
I insist on tying you down
to special times and places,
to where I think you should be.
But the whole world is your world,
not just the tiny part of it that I inhabit,
not just the familiar neighborhood
of my soul.
Surprise me, Lord,
where I least expect to find you.

# 3

It is God's love that speaks to me
in the birds and the streams
but also behind the clamor of the city.

—THOMAS MERTON

It is not just that we are tempted to confine God's presence to certain predictable times and places, it is that we think we already know what God is like and that we will instantly recognize God. "I'd know him anywhere!"

There is an old Jewish epigram that says, "God is not a kindly old uncle, he is an earthquake." It follows that if we restrict our search to looking for that kindly uncle we will most certainly overlook the earthquake—and all that lies behind the clamor of the city.

It is not only the essence of God to be beyond anything we could expect or imagine, but to shatter all our images, upset all our expectations. When we enter on the spiritual quest we need to leave behind our certainty that we already know the God we expect to encounter.

## LET US PRAY

It is easy for me
to be aware of your presence, Lord,
and to respond to you
wherever there is serenity and peace,
for that is what my soul seeks.
But I need to hear your voice
and sense your presence
in the noisy, intrusive,
demanding clamor of the city
where you are present
in the least of these,
your brothers and sisters—and mine.

# 4

In order to find myself,
I must go out of myself,
and in order to live I have to die. . . .

—THOMAS MERTON

It is very easy for us to think of our spiritual quest as a "recovery" operation, as an archaeological dig into our childhood to find and breathe new life into the dried up bones of an earlier, simpler time.

It is one more temptation to reduce the terrible mystery of God to the "familiar," to go where we have already been, to avoid the upsetting truth that the spiritual quest will take us into the unknown and the unknowable, that to live in God we will have to die to much that is familiar.

The spiritual quest is not retraced steps. It is venturing into new lands, along paths we have never walked, marked only by the footprints of those who have gone before us, and lighted by the invitation to "come follow me."

## LET US PRAY

Let me not, Lord,
cling to the things of childhood,
to comfortable, familiar ways
of finding and loving you.
I am no longer a child.
You invite me now
not to retrace my steps
but to go where I have never been.
Your invitation to come follow you
means that I must die to my childhood faith
in order to live a new life in you.
Take my hand.

# 5

The desire to find God
and to see him and to love him
is the one thing that matters.

—THOMAS MERTON

We are very fortunate indeed if never once in our childhood were we told "God sees you," with the unmistakable implication that "God will get you!"

Many people emerge from their childhood scarred with images of God that are not only frightening but repellent. Some of the images have been implanted with words and stories. But others come from experiences that are an essential part of growing up and trying to catch hold of the God we are told about. We learn about our Father in heaven from watching our fathers and mothers on earth.

We carry into our spiritual quest the good and the bad, not just religion class lessons but our personal history. In still another way we can expect that God may shatter our expectations—for the better. For only one thing matters.

## LET US PRAY

Whoever I am, however I come to you,
with whatever burdens and fears;
with whatever images I have of you,
only one thing matters:
that I truly desire to find you, to see you,
and to love you.
Break through all that stands
between my desire and you.
Set me free. Hear my prayer.
Fulfill my hope in you.

# Home

RUMI

How could the soul not take flight
When from the glorious Presence
A soft call flows sweet as honey,
comes right up to her
And whispers, "Rise up now, come away."
How could the fish not jump
Immediately from dry land into water,
When the sound of water from the ocean
Of fresh waves springs to his ear?

—RUMI

# The Unity of Love

There are always those who believe that God's soft, sweet invitation to "rise up now, to come away" is an invitation to leap beyond the human condition into an exotic spiritual world where citizenship is restricted to those who have shaken off their humanity.

It is an idea that attracts those who distrust and fear their flesh and all the limitations of creaturehood. For them spirituality is a flight from the world, from their own bodies, their own histories. They seek God in order to be other than human.

On the other hand, there are those who find in this notion an excuse to ignore the invitation to rise up and come away, for it is obviously meant not for them but for the few, the chosen, the saints.

But the great mystic poet of Islam, Rumi, is here to remind us that God's invitation is not designed to separate us from our humanity. It is, on the contrary, an ongoing call to all of us to rediscover our human roots, to come home, to return to our natural habitat. In his exquisite image, the sound of God's voice in our souls is like the irresistible sound of ocean-fresh waves to a fish stranded on dry land.

God is our natural environment, not a leap beyond the human condition but the land of our birth, our inheritance, our nourishing soil, the air we were meant to breathe—above all, the place where we are welcome.

To be with God is to be home again, to put an end to the estrangement that so many of us have come to think of as a normal existence.

Sometimes, of course, it is a matter of sin embraced and rejection fostered that keeps us far from home. But just as often, perhaps more often, it is simple ignorance of our homeland, where we have come from, where we are meant to live. It is harboring a shrunken notion of our human roots and our human destiny, a willingness to believe that God calls us to abandon our humanity rather than to put down roots, to leave our homeland rather than to embrace it.

God comes naturally to us.

God is our land, our home. For Rumi this was a central spiritual truth.

# Rumi
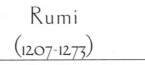
## (1207-1273)

Many believe that Muhammad Jalal al-Din, generally known today simply as Rumi but to some others as Mawlana, may be history's greatest mystical poet. He is certainly one of history's most prolific. His two most important works, *Divan-i Shams-i Tabriz* (the *Divan*) and the *Mathnavi-yi ma'navi* (the *Mathnavi*, which means "rhyming couplets") together run to more than sixty thousand verses.

He influenced not only the Moslem world but also Christianity. He still does. But it is what influenced him that makes his life and poetry especially revealing to God seekers of every age and tradition.

In 1244 he met a wandering dervish, Shams al-Din of Tabriz, who became the great love of his life and the inspiration for his great poetic work, the Divan. For two intense years they talked and prayed, danced and sang, and the brilliant young scholar ecstatically in love became a poet, the spiritual neophyte became a mystic. A profoundly human love opened his life into the divine. But the anger and jealousy of Rumi's family and students drove Shams away. He returned for a short time and married into Rumi's household, but in the end the same jealousies arose and Shams again disappeared, this time almost certainly assassinated by a member of Rumi's family.

What did not end was Rumi's love for the man who gave his name to the poet's great work, or the mystical life that it had nourished. "The Sun of Religion" had become and would remain the central divine image in Rumi's life and work. The sun does not die, it cannot die.

There is a continuity to love as there is to life. Human love is the companion of divine love, not its enemy.

God is not an escape from our humanity, but its full flowering.

In that place, we laugh ecstatically, you and I

What a miracle, you and I,
  entwined in the same nest

What a miracle, you and I,
  one love, one lover, one Fire

In this world and the next,
  in an ecstasy without end.

# I

---

Fly away, fly away bird to your native home.

—RUMI

We must go home again.

The problem is that we keep thinking we are already there, that this strange half-life is all we can hope for, that to be earthbound is our destiny, that there is no family, no friend to quench the loneliness of our souls.

But the call of God is no siren song. It is a voice rising in the deepest part of our souls, an invitation uttered in our mother tongue, reminding us that we need not be forever strangers in a strange land, that our family, our home awaits.

So let us fly, fly away home into the depths of our souls where God awaits, where questions are not asked, where we are always welcome, always awaited, where we hear and recognize our mother tongue.

## LET US PRAY

Home is
where my heart
is meant to be.
Take me home.
Let my heart speak
my mother tongue,
my soul
rediscover
its native land.

# 2

The moment we leap free of ourselves,
the wine of the friend
in all its brilliance and dazzle
is held out to us.

—RUMI

Being content with ourselves leaves us spiritually hungry.

By restricting our souls to plumbing the dry well of self-love we are left thirsting for the wine of divine friendship, our souls confined within an embrace of self-absorption that leaves us prisoner to our own small vision, our deepest appetites ignored.

We can never know God as long as we are satisfied with knowing the small world that "self" builds for us.

But the moment we "leap free" of ourselves the friendships, both human and divine, that alone can fulfill our deepest appetite, that add brilliance and dazzle to our spirits, are ours to claim. To go outside ourselves is to come home.

## LET US PRAY

Break open my heart
to make a home
large enough
to hold
the friendship
that you offer.
Give me wings
to leap free
of all that holds me
back from you.

# 3

Borrow the Beloved's eyes.
Look through them and you'll see
the Beloved's face. . . .

—RUMI

Not to see the world as God sees it is not to see the world as it truly is. It is not to recognize our home.

But most of us are content to look at the world through our own eyes, never seeing more than a reflection of our own limitations, a world made in our own image and likeness, its horizon shrunk to the narrow range of our vision, distorted by our fears and prejudices, and limited to its surface.

But more important, it is to miss the face of God, for it is only by borrowing God's eyes that we can see God's face rather than our own. It is only by looking through the eyes of God that we see what truly is in our world, in ourselves, and in the face that God has turned to us.

## LET US PRAY

Replace,
Lord God,
my eyes with yours,
so that I can see
beyond and beneath
the tiny world
I have made for myself.
Show me your face
rather than just a mirror of my own.

# 4

No heaven, no earth, just this mysterious place we walk in dazedly. . . .

—RUMI

If there are barriers separating heaven and earth, it is only because out of our desire for comfort and certitude we erect them in our souls.

We construct them hoping perhaps that if we draw a sharp distinction we will not have to walk so dazedly in the mystery of our existence. "We are here. God is there. This is for now. That is forever. This is good. That is bad." We prefer such clarity and such certitude. We prefer to travel our human journey sure-footedly, along clearly marked paths, our world and our days stretched comfortably before us.

But this is not what it means to be human. We are created to walk in mystery in a world that is neither heaven nor earth, not this, not that. Our home is a mysterious place, our destiny is to live dazedly.

## LET US PRAY

Let me not forget
that in choosing you
I have chosen
to walk in mystery,
to live
neither in heaven
nor on earth
but in you,
that mysterious place
that is my home.

# 5

When Love is in me,
I am one with Love. . . .

—RUMI

The love of which we speak, for which we seek, whose voice echoes in the deepest part of our beings, is not an object to be acquired, a reward for achievement, an adornment for our spirits. It is not something out there calling to us or even something in here that answers. It is not a thing. It is a person, a reality to be welcomed into our lives, to be embraced—to become.

To welcome the one Love into our lives is to become one with Love, that is, to become one with God and in God to exercise the oneness of Love.

When we become one with Love, we love as God loves, all that God loves, whomever God loves. We love whomever we love with the same Love that God loves.

There is no other Love, no degrees of love. There is only the one Love that we have become, who has become us.

## LET US PRAY

Let me be at home
with Love,
at ease
with one Love,
one Lover, one Fire
in this world and the next,
in an ecstasy
without end.

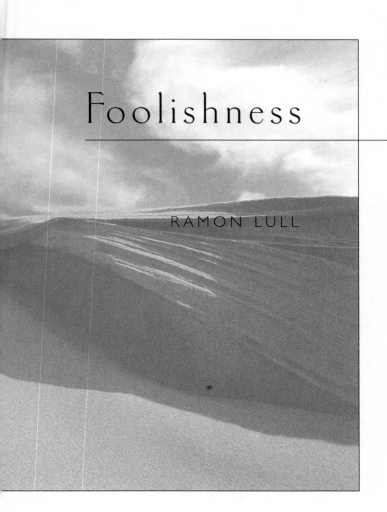

# Foolishness

### RAMON LULL

They asked the Lover, "Where do you come from?"

He answered, "From love."

"To whom do you belong?" "I belong to love."

"Who gave birth to you?" "Love."

"Where were you born?" "In love."

"Who brought you up?" "Love."

"How do you live?" "By love."

"What is your name?" "Love."

"Where do you come from?" "From love."

"Where are you going?" "To love."

"Where do you live?" "In love."

—RAMON LULL

# Foolishness

A fool, we are told, is "a person with little or no judgment, common sense, or wisdom; a silly or stupid person."

Taking God seriously requires that we turn this definition upside down even as we turn our lives inside out. Get it right, and we are "fools."

When we talk of turning the universe upside down, however, it is imperative that we avoid playing word games as we try to get at the truth of what we see to be true. Chesterton evokes an image of Francis of Assisi falling from his horse and seeing the world upside down, which was to see for the first time the world right side up. Language designed to pin down reality stumbles when it is faced with mystery, with realities that by definition elude definition.

So if we insist that what is most real and important to us is beyond language, beyond capturing, we are almost certainly going to be thought of by many as fools. We lack, they will judge, common sense. We will seem to be living in a dream world with the equivalent of childhood's "imaginary friends."

It is love that makes us fools. Not the inadequacy of love's words but what they must give way to . . . love's actions.

"Fool's" cousin, "foolhardiness," is the key to understanding what love and its actions are about.

To be "foolhardy" is to be bold or daring in a foolish way, to be rash, to be reckless. And what is more rash and reckless than to abandon the predictable, the measurable, the acceptable, and to announce that we are love's child on love's mission.

"Where do you come from?" "From love."
"Where are you going?" "To love."
"Where do you live?" "In love."
"Fool that you are!" "So be it."

# Ramon Lull
## (1232-1316)

At a time when western Christians think themselves spiritually sophisticated when they read and quote Rumi, Islam's great mystic poet, it might be a good idea to recall that seven centuries ago Ramon Lull was promoting centers for the study of Arabic and incorporating Sufic wisdom and literary forms into his writings and life.

His best known work, *The Book of the Lover and the Beloved*, is a collection of 365 aphorisms, many of which, scholars have recognized, "can be found verbatim in Arabic sources, including those of al-Ghazali."

Another of his works, *Llibre del gentil e los tres saves*, is in the form of a conversation between a Christian, a Moslem, and a Jew and is a search for common religious ground—albeit for the purpose of convincing the non-Christians of the Trinity and the incarnation.

His work, like his life, testifies not only to the universality of our human hunger for God but to the fact that the language of prayer transcends theological differences. People of various cultures and traditions find themselves easily at home in the spiritual language of other races, times, and places.

We pray together using each others' words because prayer occurs at the level where we are one, not in the world where we define ourselves by our differences.

There is an old Sufi saying readily adapted by Ramon because it captures a universal truth of our hunger for God and the way that in the end we all must take: "The ways in which the lover seeks his Beloved are long and dangerous; they are populated by meditation, sighs, and tears, and illuminated by love."

They are also populated by our common humanity and God's universal attraction.

# I

Like a fool,
the Lover went through the city
singing of his Beloved,
and men asked him if he had gone mad.

—RAMON LULL

There comes a moment for most of us when we wonder if the pursuit of God is an act of madness. The achievable, the common-sensical, is all around us. And who are we to dream what must seem, even to ourselves, the ultimate impossible dream? What arrogance!

The real problem comes when we cannot keep our dreams to ourselves. Like fools we unveil our secrets and hear others reflect back the haunting fear that has bubbled away at the back of our souls. "Are we mad?"

Almost any other confession would be better received and understood. "Get over it, girl!" "Who do you think you are?" "Get a life."

People can understand the pursuit of money or stature. We can too. What is hard, what is all but impossible to understand, is the pursuit of God by someone who otherwise seems so sane. "We don't look like fools."

## LET US PRAY

How, Lord, can I expect
others to understand
when I hardly understand myself?
This madness
is sanity.
This darkness
is light.
This absence
is presence.
This emptiness
is fulfillment.
I feel like a fool.
But only sometimes.

# 2

---

"Have you anything except love?"
"Yes," he answered,
"I have faults and have sins against my
Beloved."

—RAMON LULL

Human love forever falters on the shoals of illusion embraced and protected.

The pursuit of a divine lover, however, insistently uproots illusion, forbids closing our eyes to who we are and to the scope and demands of the love that beckons us.

Is there something in our lives other than the love we announce? There are faults. There is sin. But there are no rose-colored glasses on this journey.

We will have to do more than parrot Ramon's words.

We will have to go far beyond answering every question of the soul with easy proclamations of "love."

Love demands more than knowing the right words. . . .

## LET US PRAY

For all my brave words
I am forever, eyes closed,
stubbing my toe
on reality.
Love must go beyond words,
be rooted
in something other
than a wishing that it were so.
Here!
Untint my glasses.
Let me see clearly now,
what lies in my path.

# 3

"Tell us, Lover! Do you possess riches?"
"Yes," he replied, "I have love."
"Do you possess poverty?"
"Yes," he replied,
"because my love is not as great as it should be."

—RAMON LULL

Most of us fight day in and day out to avoid or overcome the grinding poverty of our city streets, to stay, as another generation would say, a step ahead of the sheriff, distant from the poorhouse that forever threatens from just over the hill.

We wince at the sight of millions of children starving to death on the 6 o'clock news. But when it comes to praying we are very good at stifling reality with glib words. . . .

But only at that moment when we really accept that our wealth is in the love of God and our poverty in its lack, do we move beyond "spiritually correct" words into lived life where all our accustomed values are turned upside down and inside out. However terrifying that might be.

## LET US PRAY

Let me pray,
at least this once,
without glibness,
roughly,
stutteringly.
Let the very hesitancy of my words
reveal the true poverty of my soul,
the honesty
of my desire
for riches
only you can give.

# 4

The trials and sorrows for which Love gets blamed, are the growing pains of love itself.

—RAMON LULL

Growing toward the divine Beloved is as painful, as demanding, as uncomfortable as growth itself. Only more so. It's not the way we want it or in the lap of comforting prayer and dreaming, the way we hoped it would be.

It is not a burrowing into warmth while life happens around us. It is a stretching process in which we are forever shedding our own confining skins, leaving behind shells which we have grown used to, our protective coloring useless against Love's blazing light.

Don't blame Love for making love so hard.

It could not be otherwise so long as love demands growth rather than a lifetime of nursery warmth, so long as we choose life with Love.

## LET US PRAY

I will not blame you, Love,
for making love so hard.
How could it be otherwise?
It is not easy
to do what love requires,
to leave the walled city
of my soul
for a life with you,
to abandon
the security
I have come to rely on
for the unpredictability
of Love itself.

# 5

If we do not understand each other in speech,
we can make ourselves understood by love.

—RAMON LULL

"I wonder," we sometimes think, "if I shall ever be able
to tell someone who I am or what it is that I feel about
them."

Words, we come to accept, are never enough when it
really matters, when we reach out to understand and
be understood. When we pray.

Not even words of love.

Only love itself. And not a love that begins and ends in
warm feelings, but a love that speaks in wordless
courage, in patience and kindness, that is neither
boastful nor jealous, arrogant nor rude, that bears all
things, that believes all things, that endures all things.

That speaks by being, by doing. . . .

## LET US PRAY

Hear, Lord, not my words,
not even my best words,
not even my most prayerful words.
Listen to my life.
Let my actions speak.
Awkward as I may be,
let me act out of love,
wary of boasting and jealousy,
content to speak humbly.

# More

## GREGORY OF NYSSA

The soul,
having gone out at the word of her Beloved,
looks for him
but does not find him.
She calls on him,
though he cannot be reached
by any word,
and she is told by the watchmen
that she is in love with the unattainable,
and that the object of her love
cannot be apprehended.
But the veil of her grief is lifted
when she learns that the object of her desire
consists of constantly going on with her quest
and never ceasing in her ascent. . . .

—GREGORY OF NYSSA

# More

Gregory would say that on the spiritual journey we move forever from glory to glory, even after death, even in eternity; that there is no final satisfying glory, no resting place.

We want to believe the opposite.

We want to believe that when we speak of God hunger, we are talking about the first movements of our desire, the first steps on our path, that the hunger we feel is a passing phase, a pang that will be erased, an ache that will give way to satisfaction.

But there is never enough for the soul.

Every taste of God only deepens our hunger, leaving us with a greater need for more.

This is not easy to accept because it requires of us that we turn our expectations upside down.

We are asked to commit to a journey that will never get "there." We will always be en route.

We will be asked to live with a hunger that will not ease, but only grow.

What we have will never be enough. We will never have it all.

For we are in love with the unattainable. The object of our love cannot be apprehended.

The object of our desire consists of constantly going on with our quest, never ceasing in our ascent.

# Gregory of Nyssa
## (335-395)

His father was a saint (Basil the elder), so was his sister (Macrina), and so, too, were two brothers (Basil the Great and Peter of Sebate).

But for a while it appeared that Gregory had other plans. He was much more interested in the fashionable paganism of the Roman Emperor, Julian the Apostate, marriage, and a career as a rhetorician. His brother Basil also had plans for him. He appointed him a bishop, and Gregory took his first steps in a distinguished career as a church administrator, apologist, and theologian. But this was not to be his legacy. In his later years, with his church careers behind him, he created two great works that established him, in the eyes of many, as the founder of Christian mystical theology.

His *Commentary on the Song of Songs* and his *Life of Moses* established him as a powerfully original voice who could draw on and color his commitment to orthodox Christianity with insights from Greek philosophy and Jewish mysticism.

But there is no question that it was his immersion in scripture that gives his work its originality and lasting influence.

In our own times the study of scripture is dominated by flyspecking the texts for historical authenticity. The linguists and historians carry the day. But for Gregory the sacred texts were above all else a mystical treasury that plots and illumines the ascendance of the soul to union with God. It is an approach that today is greeted with more than a little suspicion but one that in the hands of someone such as Gregory becomes a source of illumination on what he himself calls a journey into darkness.

But perhaps most important, as one of eastern Christianity's strongest voices, his wisdom softens the often unremitting, cautious rationalism of the west, its unease with the poetry of revelation.

# I

The infinite beauty of God is constantly being discovered anew.

—GREGORY OF NYSSA

Each new glimpse of God is like discovering him for the first time because none of our efforts to tie down, to cling to what is infinite, is of the least avail.

"You cannot capture lightning in a jar," we were told as children. But part of our hearts goes on trying to capture God's beauty in a word, a phrase, or a treasured image. His lightning brilliance flashes through the darkness, but for only a second. And when the lightning comes again it is something completely new.

His beauty is ever ancient, ever new, never twice the same.

Gregory adds that God's beauty "is always seen as something new and strange when compared with what the mind has already understood."

There is always "more." And the more is always new.

## LET US PRAY

Help me
not to settle
for what I have,
for what comes too easily
to my heart,
but to seek
in every passing moment
the "more"
you have promised.
O beauty ever ancient,
ever new,
you are never twice the same.
You are always a surprise
to the heart that is ready
for you.
I am ready
for more of you.

# 2

How can that which is invisible reveal itself in the night?

—GREGORY OF NYSSA

The night strips away the surface of the world.

But only if we surrender to its darkness can we see what is always there, waiting for us behind the sunlit brilliance of the day.

The night is rich with God who waits to be heard in its silence, waits to be seen in its shadows.

But we are tempted to fill up its silence with a thousand other, less demanding voices, tempted to banish the shadows with day-bright images.

We are, to be honest, far more comfortable with a burning bush than the cloudiness of the journey, or the dark at the mountain's top.

"I have been here all along," says night's voice, "but you have to leave the day behind."

## LET US PRAY

Loosen day's grip
on my heart and imagination,
O Lord,
and let me surrender my heart
to the night
where free of day's images
I can see your face.
Strip away
the face of the world
with all its false light
and glittering promises
and lead me
into the darkness
where in the fullness of your mystery
you are waiting.

# 3

Truth stands outside the doors
of our souls . . . and knocks.

—GREGORY OF NYSSA

The knock comes, but we don't hear it.

We're in a back room and the sound doesn't carry.

We're talking with someone else.

We've deliberately shut ourselves off to get on with life, to stay on schedule.

We weren't expecting anyone anyway, so we are not properly dressed to answer the knock.

It may be just another pamphleteering evangelist.

"I thought I heard a knock. I must have been wrong."

Wait a while. They'll go away.

## LET US PRAY

It seems
that you must knock
very loudly
to catch my attention.
Something else,
someone else, anything else,
anyone else
has an easier time
catching my ear.
I am busy
about many things
when only one thing matters.
Please knock again.
Here in the silence of the night
I am listening.
Speak, Lord, your servant is listening.

# 4

She leaves all that can be grasped
by sense or reason.

—GREGORY OF NYSSA

If indeed we answer the knock, it seems important to us that we carry with us all our defenses. We go dressed for the occasion, we look our Sunday best, we are careful to make clear that we need nothing. We prepare our answers and line them up like ducks in a row.

"We gave at church."

To be empty-handed is not our style.

But it is what God looks for—a humble acknowledgment that sense and reason are not enough for this journey, not right for this meeting.

It is not the time or place to present résumés of our spiritual achievements. In the end they count for nothing. What we leave behind is what recommends us.

Our task is not to impress the One who knocks but simply to open the door.

## LET US PRAY

Let me close the door on this day
on the world where I must prove myself
again and again.
Let me enter this night
and your presence
with empty hands
and know that you ask
no more of me.
This is not the time
or place
to prove my qualifications for your love.
I need not qualify,
I can't.
But I can accept.
I do.

MONKS OF MT. TABOR

# 5

It is sufficient if Truth merely whets our knowledge with some meager and obscure ideas. . . .

—GREGORY OF NYSSA

Even our best ideas of God are "meager and obscure." So if we look for and expect to find God only in life-shattering moments, we will almost surely miss the sound of his knock.

God comes not just when he has been invited and we are on our best behavior but at odd, unexpected moments of his choosing.

If we wait for dramatic revelations we will miss every day's meager and obscure insights.

We will miss what is sufficient. We will miss his quiet voice, the simple moments of truth.

Every little bit of life, every small insight whets our appetite for the "more" our souls forever desire and seek.

There's more to everything we see, and that more is God's presence just below the surface of our world.

## LET US PRAY

There was more
to every moment of this day
that I missed,
busy as I was
waiting for some great surprise,
some dramatic moment.
If I will take the time
to scratch the surface of my day,
you will be there,
even as you are now,
in the final moments of this day,
in the quiet of this night.
Speak.
I will be listening.

# Dying

## FRANCIS OF ASSISI

O Divine Master,
grant that I may
not so much seek to be consoled
as to console,
to be understood
as to understand,
to be loved
as to love.
For it is in giving
that we receive,
it is in pardoning
that we are pardoned,
and it is in dying
that we are born to eternal life.

—FRANCIS OF ASSISI

# Dying

The most devilish temptation facing anyone seeking a spiritual life is not the drama of flamboyant sin conquered but the quiet seduction of self-centered isolation.

We feel the pull of retreating from the world—from other people—of finding a haven of gentle, uninvolved serenity, the ultimate "warm-fuzzy."

"Excuse me, please, while I crawl inside myself and call it holiness."

God looks like a way of getting away from it all.

But life in God is not an escape route, not life in a cocoon, but an insistent ongoing demand to move outside ourselves, to reverse the direction of our lives from hiding to involvement, to doing for others what we are tempted to reserve for ourselves.

It is not basking in the warm luxury of being understood but reaching out to understand, not so much seeking consolation but reaching out to console, pardoning others, all others, when the soft side of our souls would like to settle for being pardoned.

Francis calls the choice by its right name: dying.

We've got a lot of dying to do if we are to have the lives our souls hunger for, a lot of entering into the great mystery of death and resurrection.

Suddenly the "sweet" Franciscan prayer takes on an edge. It is no longer easy to muffle its final words.

# Francis of Assisi
## (1181-1226)

So many of us who are comfortable with a garden statue of St. Francis would be extremely uncomfortable if a very-much-alive Francis were to join us in that same serene garden setting.

The conversation, we instinctively know, would not begin and end with seed packet comparisons.

His biography is the best of all antidotes to the saccharine image that disguises his message.

He was a rich kid who became poor, not as a one-time gesture, not as a romantic metaphor, but as a lifelong choice reinforced daily by a relentless effort to have ever less.

He was a street person who begged for his food, who convinced others to do the same, and who was the first to send packing would-be followers who chose "more" over "less."

He was scruffy and unkempt. His idea of living was dying to the world from which he came and which was all around him to the day he died—the world which most of us cling to, terrified of losing.

He lived only forty-five years.

He was at home with Brother Sun and Sister Moon, but his chosen family was brother and sister leper, brother and sister needy.

Nearly 800 years after his death he remains one of the best loved spiritual teachers of all times, revered now perhaps more than ever, and not just among believers but universally.

It would be too bad if the gentle figure of our gardens, with its congregation of birds and animals, were to displace completely the demanding figure that unsettled the conscience of the medieval world.

It is important not to mute his life and words, softening them to our liking and our comfort, for it is in dying that we are born to eternal life.

# I

It is in giving
that we receive. . . .

—FRANCIS OF ASSISI

It may no longer be fashionable or socially correct to proclaim that "greed is good." But it's still all right to live that way, still all right to subscribe, discreetly of course, to that other bit of movie wisdom that the person who "ends up with the most toys wins."

So to accept the word of Francis that it is better to give than receive, we have to break with a culture that is all around us. We have to die to the reigning gospel of our times that we are what we possess.

To convert the center of our lives from receiving to giving is a kind of dying, a kind of conversion from a life of accumulation and consumption to a life where things are put in their place.

Francis lived his own wisdom: he gave away all that he possessed to receive what only God can give.

## LET US PRAY

It is not that I want the world, Lord,
but there is still a part of me
that believes
that with just a little more
I would be content.
There is still a part of me
that says if I were blessed
with just a little more
I could afford to be generous.
Help me to share
the little that I have,
to know with Francis
the joy of letting go,
of placing my trust in you
and not in what I possess.

# 2

It is in pardoning
that we are pardoned. . . .

—FRANCIS OF ASSISI

That we expect to be unquestionably and fully forgiven even our most obnoxious behavior goes without saying.

But forgiving the behavior of others, if we are honest, comes much too quickly to our tongues and much too slowly to our hearts.

We, of course, deserve pardon by God and humans; everyone else can expect to pay the full toll for their behavior.

But in the world of Francis forgiveness is promised only to those who are forgiving, and to forgive we must die to every lingering, cherished hurt of our souls, forgetting even as we forgive.

We must forgive those who trespass even as we ask forgiveness for our trespasses.

## LET US PRAY

My Father
who art in heaven,
I ask you so easily
to forgive me
as I forgive others,
but I'm afraid
that you will take me at my word.
It is so hard for me to forgive,
almost impossible, it seems,
to forget.
Help me
to erase from my memory
every lingering hurt,
every unforgiven moment
that stands between me
and your unqualified forgiveness.

Bless me with the grace
to forgive
so that one day soon
you can take me at my word.

# 3

. . . not so much seek to be consoled
as to console. . . .

—FRANCIS OF ASSISI

No one of us over a lifetime escapes moments of loss
that threaten our ability, our will to go on.

We lose someone we love, someone who has given
shape and meaning to our lives. Or we lose our health
or our desire to live. Perhaps our trust is betrayed.

We look for someone to console us, to comfort and
soothe us, to offer solace. But most of all we look for
someone to restore hope to us in the midst of our pain.
For our greatest loss would be the loss of hope. And the
greatest gift would be its restoration.

We seek to be consoled.

But our calling is to console, to give the gift of hope,
when no other gift is enough, to share the hope that is
in us with someone who is in danger of losing it.

## LET US PRAY

The greatest of your gifts,
O Lord,
is the gift of hope,
the quiet belief
that there is a tomorrow
worth living for,
that the pain we feel today
is not all there is.
What greater gift
could we give another
than a moment of hope
when everything worth living for
seems lost.
You are my hope.
Help me not so much
to look for consolation
as to console.

# 4

Seek not so much to be understood
as to understand. . . .

—FRANCIS OF ASSISI

There is no more effective way out of our own loneliness than letting others know that they are not alone.

"I understand," we say and hope that somehow this simple phrase will bridge the mysterious, irreducible distance between two people.

If, however, by "understanding" we mean "comprehension," we don't understand at all. No one can ever really enter the soul of another. No two people have ever experienced their lives, their world, and their God in exactly the same way.

What we mean is that we are reaching out in empathy, in sympathy, in rapport.

"You are not alone," we say. And suddenly neither are we.

## LET US PRAY

More than anything else, Lord,
I want to hear you say, "You are not alone.
I am with you always,
even to the end of time."

We need, Lord,
to hear from others, too,
that we are not alone in this world.
But even as we desire to be understood,
we need to reach out in understanding.
Like us, our friends, our family,
and those we meet along the way
long to hear:
"You are not alone.
God is with you.
So am I."

Let them hear it from me.
Let them hear it without having to ask.

# 5

It is in dying
that we are born to eternal life.

—FRANCIS OF ASSISI

A new, fuller life is what spirituality is all about.

And dying to our old lives, our present lives, our old
and present ways of living and doing things, our old
and present attitudes, is its price.

And the price is not negotiable. We can't buy it
wholesale. There are no two-for-one offers or "this
week only" bargains.

Some part of us has to die if we are to live. And the part
of us that must go will not be some extra that we could
easily and joyfully do without. It will certainly be
something that we are clinging to with all our energy
because we have come to believe that it is the source of
our happiness, our lives.

Be prepared to let go, to die a little every day.

## LET US PRAY

The life I know
always seems
better than the life I don't know,
but the life, Lord,
that I don't yet have
is the life I want,
a life fuller, richer,
a life with you.

So teach me how to die
one small death at a time,
so that I might wake
to the fuller life
you have promised.

# Unknowing

ANGELUS SILESIUS

Not spirit and not light,
not one, truth, unity,
not what we call divine,
not reason, and not wisdom,
not goodness, love or will,
no thing, no nothing either,
not being or concern.
He is what I or we,
or any other creature
has never come to know
before we were created.

—ANGELUS SILESIUS

# Mystery

We know and generally accept that in our everyday experience there is much that we do not understand. But for the most part we go on our way presuming that with enough time, with enough smarts, with enough luck—with enough research funding—there are no unanswerable questions, no unsolvable problems, no puzzles beyond our human capacity to unravel.

We presume to the point of certainty that sooner or later scientists will discover the cures for cancer, AIDS, and the "common cold." Someday—sooner or later—with telescopes or computers or other tools as yet uncreated or even undreamed, we will come to know how the earth began and whether or not there is "life" on one of those millions of planets that remain tantalizingly just beyond our present reach.

We live for the most part in a world of the known, the ignored, the forgotten, the yet to be discovered—in a world of problems posed, problems solved. But our hunger for God originates in and takes us to another place, to a world of something else. Something more. To a reality whose truth goes beyond solvable problems and unraveled puzzles, whose existence goes beyond what we can see and measure, whose importance is precisely in that it escapes our finitude.

There is something that beckons us on, that we feel compelled to explore knowing that we shall never fully exhaust it, never completely comprehend it.

Our spiritual quest, we come to understand, is a journey into the realm of the unknowable.

No one has better understood the centrality of mystery to our spiritual growth than Angelus Silesius, who gave new life to one of western mysticism's oldest traditions.

# Angelus Silesius
## (1624-1677)

From the earliest centuries there has been a mystical tradition that is called the negative way. Briefly, it means that no human words, no concepts however subtle, no images however searching are up to the task of describing God. The best we can do is to approach God in what God is not.

We may call God Lord, or Father, or Wisdom, but he (she) is none of these. Not even spirit, not light, not even divine. God is not a "thing," but neither is God "no-thing."

We find God not in light but in darkness, not in his presence but in his absence.

This was the way of the man who would in the course of a relatively short life publish some of the most striking and enduring spiritual literature of his time. He was born Johannes Scheffler in Breslau, the capital of Silesia (what is now southwest Poland). He entered a world caught up in the anguish and bitter religious polemics of the Counter Reformation, and embroiled in the wrenching struggles of the Thirty Years War. Perhaps as a response to the massive confusion and pain of the times—a time not unlike our own—it was a period in which spirituality blossomed.

Scheffler, who had an extraordinary education in at least three European universities and who could boast of a combined doctorate in medicine and philosophy, left his court appointment and chose a life of the spirit and a new name, Angelus Silesius. His *Cherubinic Wanderer* is a timeless collection of poems and aphoristic couplets, a form immensely popular at the time and ideally suited to the paradoxical, almost Zen-like character of his spiritual insights. Their pointed brevity and wit mirror the uncapturable mystery of God, illuminating the spiritual quest with quick lightning flashes, even as they provide easily memorized verses that anyone can carry with him or her through the day.

His writing conveys in its special form that our hunger for God is always about the pursuit of mystery and the finitude of our words.

# I

God is the purest naught,
untouched by time or space;
The more we reach for him,
the more he will escape.

—ANGELUS SILESIUS

The spiritual quest is fraught with paradox because it is a journey into mystery, a pursuit of what in the end is beyond any of our human capacities to comprehend. Any attempt to capture God with our words or to contain God within our categories is not only doomed to failure, it is fundamentally to misunderstand the reason for our journey.

We know only what God is not. We will never fully know what God is. We know, for example, that for however long or however often we use the masculine pronoun, God is not a "He." Nor is God a "She." God escapes gender as surely as he/she escapes all our other needs to define the object of our quest.

## LET US PRAY

Help me, Lord,
to begin my quest for you,
knowing and accepting
that you will forever escape
my every attempt to confine you
to what I can understand.
My words cannot capture you.
My imagination cannot define you.
My heart cannot limit you.
But support me, I beg you,
on this journey without end,
with a love that knows no limits.

# 2

God is that which he is;
I am that which I am;
and if you know one well,
you know both me and him.

—ANGELUS SILESIUS

Silesius reminds us that it is not just God that is a mystery. We, too, have as the heart of our beings a core of reality that will forever escape definition or confinement. We have been made in God's image.

Even as God is not just a "so far unsolved" problem, we are not hanks of hair, bags of bones, ongoing collections of experiences subject to final analysis.

Our spiritual quest is an exploration of our likeness to God—a case of mystery courting mystery. We are in search of the only reality worthy of our efforts, the only truth large enough to satisfy our deepest needs.

## LET US PRAY

It is because
you have made me, Lord,
in your image and likeness
that my soul seeks you
and will not rest until it rests in you.
Even as you are not
the sum of your words and images,
neither am I.
Help me, Lord, not to settle
for anything less
than the divine mystery
you have made of me.

# 3

The abyss that is my soul
invokes unceasingly
The abyss that is my God.

—ANGELUS SILESIUS

Abyss . . . such a strange, unexpected word for our souls and for our God. It conjures up images of the land dropping suddenly away from where we stand secure and certain of our footing. Another step and we could plunge over the edge of what we know into a vast, bottomless darkness, or into immeasurable light—a headlong journey without end.

Abyss is a synonym for what lies in wait for us beyond what we know.

The spiritual quest invites us to surrender the security of what we know, what we can measure, and what we can exhaust for the deepest, unknown reality of our mysterious being, and the even more mysterious reality of God.

## LET US PRAY

It would be easier, Lord,
to stay with what I know,
to take only well-marked paths
to familiar places
in my heart and soul.
But if I am to come to you
then I must leave behind
the comfort of what I already know
and accept your invitation
to journey into your infinite mystery.
Take my hand,
guide my steps,
give courage to my heart and soul.

# 4

What Cherubim may know
will never bring me peace,
Outstrip I must all thought,
the highest goal to reach.

—ANGELUS SILESIUS

God does not play a game of "catch me if you can." God is not a tease, forever disappearing around corners, through doorways, into blind alleys, amused at our frustration, laughing at the folly of our dreaming dreams of meeting him face to face.

Rather, God meets us and embraces us where we are, takes us by the hand, leading us beyond the limitations of our own thoughts, the inadequacy of our own words, and even the wisdom of angels, bringing us a step at a time closer and closer to our goal of living in the mystery and presence of God.

## LET US PRAY

Not even what your angels know
is meant to be, Lord,
enough to satisfy the hunger for you
that you have created in my soul.
Meet me where I am.
Lead me beyond
the limitations of my words
and the poverty of my spirit.
Let nothing but you satisfy me.
Draw me step by step closer to you
and deeper into the mystery
of your life without end.

# 5

What men have said of God,
not yet suffices me,
My life and light is One
beyond divinity.

—ANGELUS SILESIUS

None of the words we use about God—even the word God, even the word divinity—defines God, but acts only as so many arrows pointing to a great mystery that defies all our words.

They are something—necessary, inevitable, and marvelous achievements of our deepest humanity.

But they are not enough.

With Silesius our souls ache for the "One" who is beyond "divinity"—beyond what we can name. Having the right words is no substitute for experiencing the light and life to which our words can only point.

## LET US PRAY

In the beginning was the "Word"
and the word was with you,
and the word was you.
Nothing we can ever say of you,
no words that we can ever craft,
will ever be enough,
will ever substitute for the Word
that is, was, and ever will be you.
But we must go on forming words
in which to search for you.
Accept the love and hope, Lord,
with which we pray them.

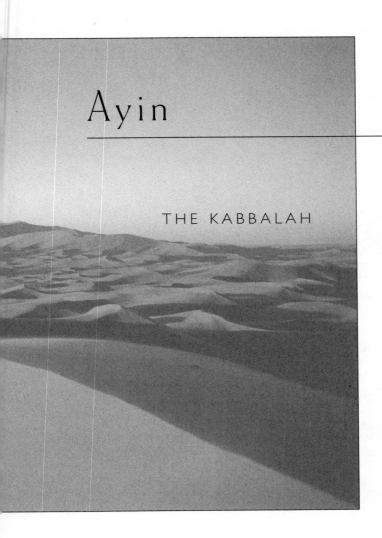

# Ayin

## THE KABBALAH

If we are attached
to the material
nature of the world—
If we think of ourselves
as something,
then God cannot
clothe his self in us,
for God is infinite.
No vessel can contain God,
unless we think of ourselves
as Ayin.

—THE KABBALAH

# Nothingness

The spiritual journey begins and ends in nothingness.

The rich mystical tradition of Judaism, Kabbalah, has a word for this nothingness. It is Ayin.

Our journey begins in Ayin because it demands of us that we recognize that everything we cling to, everything by which we measure our reality, everything that gives us a sense of control, everything that we can name, and above all the words with which we name them, is nothing, that their total is nothingness.

It is to call everything that we have come to rely on by its true name, Ayin, nothingness, and to accept and embrace it in its very nothingness.

As long as we are attached to the material nature of the world, as long as we think of ourselves as something, and the world as something, then God cannot begin his work in us, cannot take up his dwelling in us. There is no room for him. It is only by seeing ourselves as nothingness, as Ayin, that we make room for he who is infinite.

And here is the irony: Ayin, nothingness, is also a word for God. Every other name is an attempt to capture what cannot be caught with our most subtle words, our most exquisite reasoning.

God is Ayin not because he is limited but because he is boundless.

God is what cannot be defined. He is nothing that we know, nothing that we can name or control.

He is no-thing. He is no-thing-ness. But he is not nothing, for "nothing" is as confining as "thing," as any other word which we seek to surround and comprehend, to grasp, to seize the twin mysteries of our own reality and the reality of God.

Beware, however. This embrace of nothingness is no word game for lazy afternoons or late-night verbal jousting, no semantic journey of the mind, but a treacherous plunging of the soul into the unnamable depths of its own mystery and the mystery of God.

It demands, as the Kabbalah instructs, that we think of ourselves as Ayin and forget ourselves totally. Only then can we transcend time, and space, and differences.

But heed the warning of Kabbalah: "Be careful! Keep your soul from gazing and your mind from conceiving, lest you drown."

## The Kabbalah

The Kabbalah came together in the twelfth century in a community of traditional Jewish scholars, lawyers, and mystics. Unlike other western traditions, however, in which the mystical record is dominated by personal testaments, the Kabbalah is a literature of communal wisdom.

Until recently, in the name of protecting the young from the potentially treacherous shoals of mysticism, it was a wisdom forbidden to any but the mature; young Jews were warned off. Some said you should be twenty years of age, others said forty, for to enter into Kabbalah is to embrace fire. Only the spiritually mature, those with a background of rabbinical learning, who are sound mentally and emotionally, and preferably married, need apply.

In words that apply to every tradition, Kabbalah scholar Daniel C. Matt reminds us that: "Mystical teachings are enticing, powerful, and potentially dangerous. The spiritual seeker soon discovers that he or she is not exploring something 'up there,' but rather the beyond that lies within. Letting go of traditional notions of God and self can be both liberating and terrifying."

Kabbalah, born as some say in the primeval innocence of Eden and nourished in the Provençal village where it was first published, spread in time into Spain and the whole Mediterranean world, picking up along the way traces of the same Neo-Platonism that was an increasingly significant part of both Christian and Islamic-Sufi mystical learning and extending its own influence into the literature of the Renaissance. By the seventeenth century there was, in fact, a Christian Kabbalistic literature. In a relatively short period the original small pamphlets swelled to a vast work called The Holy Zohar, which is to this day the canon—the body of laws—of Kabbalah. Over the centuries it has become not only the mystical wisdom most closely associated with Judaism but an influence on mystics of every tradition and a presence in popular spiritual literature.

The themes of Kabbalah are many and profound, but none strikes closer to the hunger of the struggling soul than its understanding of how for our comfort we diminish God to limits set by our own spiritual poverty and in the process undermine the possibility of faith itself.

It warns us of the danger of clinging, for example, to an image of God as an old man with white hair. "Imagining this and similar fantasies, the fool corporealizes God. He falls into one of the traps that destroy faith. His awe of God is limited by his imagination."

# I

What we can do
is strive to pursue true knowledge.

—THE KABBALAH

True knowledge begins where knowing ends.

We can pursue it only if we are willing to journey beyond the edge of comfort; willing to choose to have our lives upset, destabilized, reversed; willing to shatter our trust in the ground on which we walk; willing to overthrow and abandon our expectations of what is real and dependable.

It is to let go of things in order to uncover the no-thing that we most deeply are and to embrace the ultimate no-thing that awaits us beyond our comprehension.

But it is something that we can do. It is within our realm of possibility because it is our deepest destiny, the ultimate realization of ourselves. God does not call us to the impossible.

## LET US PRAY

Deliver me, God,
from the temptation
of accepting the world
that I see
as the only world that is.
For the world that I see
is not the world for which you created me.
Give strength
to my pursuit of true knowledge
life lived in your presence,
in your mystery.

# 2

The effort consists of removing ourselves
from the material aspect of things. . . .

—THE KABBALAH

We live in a material world that can be captured by our senses, and it is easy to be content here. But to discover and inhabit the world for which we have been created we need to journey beneath and beyond the material surface of things.

The senses tell us about things. But about no-thing which we are, which God is, they can tell us nothing except what we are not, what God is not.

To get to no-thing we have to abandon all the things that disguise and overlay the spiritual reality for which we were created and for which we seek.

It is not a question of despising the material world, which is the land of our search, but of acknowledging that what we have at hand is not any thing compared to what we seek.

## LET US PRAY

Peel away,
I ask of you,
the world that solicits my trust,
until there is nothing there but you.
Give me new footing
to replace the ground
on which I have walked till now.
Letting go of every thing
let me come to the no-thing
that I am, that you are.

# 3

Ultimately holiness is a gift.

—THE KABBALAH

There is no earning our spiritual keep, no paying our way into the presence of God, no qualifying for divine acceptance.

The slightest taste of God is a gift. We are carried on God's shoulders over even the shortest distance and never enter God's presence able to claim that our merit has brought us there.

To know this is the beginning of spiritual wisdom. To accept it is already to be on the path to holiness.

To be persons of faith, hope, and charity, of generosity and compassion, of truthfulness and fidelity is to be expected of us, but no amount of finite virtue can earn the infinite love of God.

Holiness is always a gift.

## LET US PRAY

I come empty handed,
bringing to you
nothing but my desire
to receive your gifts.
Fill my soul.

# 4

---

In the end, the Blessed Holy One
will guide us on the path. . . .

—THE KABBALAH

The thought of journeying into mystery, of leaving behind the world we know for a universe where the values and expectations of a lifetime are overthrown can paralyze the soul and vaporize our dreams.

But only if we believe that we must make the journey alone, traveling through unmapped territory with no guide but our good will, with nothing to rely on but our own devices, dependent solely on our own strengths.

Such is not the case. God may insist that we take the first step, but "in the end, the Blessed Holy One will guide us on the path."

God is not just the object of our journey, but our companion on the way, our guide through lands of the soul where we have never been and where God does not expect us to chart our own path or travel alone.

## LET US PRAY

Come,
take me by the hand
and lead me beyond my fears
into the place of mystery,
of no-thing-ness,
where alone
the dreams you have planted in my soul
can come true.

# 5

We become a dwelling place of the divine.

—THE KABBALAH

The goal of our journey is to become a dwelling place of God.

But here is the test, the condition, the paradox of what we seek: We can never become the dwelling place of God so long as we think of ourselves as a dwelling place, as something, as anything. "If we think of ourselves as something, then God cannot clothe his self in us, for God is infinite."

Because nothing is big enough to shelter the presence of God, we must become no-thing. We cannot "contain God, unless we think of ourselves as Ayin."

Our seemingly unquenchable desire to be something, to become someone, forever gets in the way of becoming what God means us to be—vessels whose very no-thing-ness leaves room for his presence.

## LET US PRAY

Save me
from the trap
that destroys faith
by limiting you
to what I can imagine,
to what I can conceive.
Let me not forget
that it is only
by accepting my no-thing-ness
and yours
that I can leave room for you in my life.

# Passion

## HILDEGARD OF BINGEN

We have not
surrendered our lives to bloodless evil,
but neither are we
in fiery pursuit of goodness.
We stare into an abyss
so deep that we cannot glimpse its bottom,
and at the same time raise our eyes to mountain tops
that are unreachable.
And we stand between them
wavering, unsettled and uncommitted.

—HILDEGARD OF BINGEN

# Passion

Like the lovers that all the world loves, those who have fallen in love with God—the mystics—are passionate, ardent, single-minded in their yearning to be at one with the object of their love. They do nothing by halves.

Nothing, therefore, subverts the spiritual quest more than attempting the journey with only half a heart, harboring the hope that life in God's presence is synonymous with undemanding serenity and that the path to God leads away from the disappointing, demanding, dangerously ambiguous world of human experience and into the protective arms of comfort, consolation, and certainty.

God lives outside the comfort zone, beyond hedged bets, in risks accepted, in dangers embraced.

Access to his presence is limited to a passionate heart.

Many of us, however, beg off an ardent pursuit of God in the name of common sense and moderation. Cool is the measure of our sanity and our sophistication. We have been taught to settle for safety and security. So we move to the center, to the level plain with its guardrails, and try to avert our eyes from the abyss that opens at our feet and from the mountain that invites us to ascend beyond our sight. We cling to the vain hope that God rewards timidity.

We spend our days and drain our energy, as Hildegard says, "wavering, unsettled and uncommitted." But fainthearted, drained of spiritual passion, we are pale shadows of what we could be, of what we are meant to be.

Only a passionate heart can break through the fences of our cultivated fears and cosseted timidities and open up our lives to the extravagant love of God and the uncharted, unpredictable adventure of the spiritual journey.

Only a passionate heart can overcome our fear of heights, our preference for solid, familiar ground beneath our feet. And only a passionate heart can overcome our fear of failure, our taste for certainty, the security of paths already walked, and the lingering memories of mediocrity's comfort.

We ignore at our own risk the harsh, scriptural voice: "I know your works: you are neither cold nor hot. Would that you were cold or hot! But because you are lukewarm, I will spew you out of my mouth."

Only a passionate heart need apply.

# Hildegard of Bingen
## (1098-1179)

Such was the heart of Hildegard of Bingen.

It was passion that took her, a twelfth-century nun, in directions and to heights that were daring and even dangerous for a woman of her times, and for that matter, for women of many generations that have followed her but which only now are discovering her.

There was in her, first of all, a passion for knowledge. At a time when it was commonplace to say that the world of scholarship was unsuited to the inferior brain of a woman, she wrote an encyclopedia of the natural sciences and other books on animals, herbs, trees, gems, and metals. She was a living treasure chest of folklore and herbal medicine.

She was an accomplished playwright and composer who believed passionately that harmony was such a great blessing that in her drama she denies music to the devil, of all God's creatures the only one unworthy of its beauty. Today her drama is performed throughout the world and her music is played, recorded, and broadcast in the most sophisticated settings.

Living at a time when the church and society as a whole were riven not just with mediocrity and spiritual indifference but with abuses that cut away at the very roots of Christianity, there was also in her a passion for political and religious reform. She wrote constantly to bishops, popes, and rulers calling them back to the service of God. And she preached at every opportunity the absolute necessity of deep reform, tweaking the clergy with the charge that things had gotten so bad that it took a woman, inferior though her sex might be, to speak the truth and institute reform.

But strongest of all was her visionary passion for the mysteries of God. Unlike most mystics her spirituality was dominated not by a perfect sense of union with God but by an extraordinary series of visions that she recorded in several volumes—detailed, brilliantly colorful, complex visions of the history of God and his creatures, from the fall of the angels to the final days of the world and the race.

The point of this, however, is not that she was passionate about so many things but that passion was the characteristic virtue of her spirituality, a passion that is never a synonym for warm sentimentality but always a word for courage, risk, and adventure, for full-heartedness, for life lived with burning intensity.

# I

We are like mild, soft winds that blow
but bring no nourishment to any living thing.

—HILDEGARD OF BINGEN

The dry, late-afternoon, mild, soft breeze brushing against our skin is a welcome relief to the heat of the day, but it brings nothing to a drought-desiccated land. It carries no nourishment where it is needed, absorbing instead what moisture is left. It touches only the surface.

What is needed is a storm—hard, persistent, pelting rain that can penetrate the dry crust of the earth and reach what traces of life still struggle beneath the surface, even though it will almost certainly uproot whatever traces of half-life cling tenuously to the surface of the land.

God may come to us, of course, in soft gentle breezes that refresh the surface of our lives, but we shouldn't count on it. He comes to nourish our parched souls, and that demands the full force of his love—strong, penetrating, persistent, and uprooting.

## LET US PRAY

There is within me, Lord,
a dryness
that will not surrender to gentle touches.
I need the full strength of your love,
however demanding it may be,
if you are to crack open the surface of my life
to nourish the other life
that struggles to be born
at the center of my soul.

# 2

We begin but we do not finish.

—HILDEGARD OF BINGEN

Always, it seems that we shall be able to touch the face of God just one step beyond where we are. With each step his features become clearer, deeper, richer—at one moment more inviting, at the next more demanding. But each step requires, whether it is our first or our fiftieth, that we take still another. We know deep within us that however far we have come our spirits have not yet arrived where we want to be. The face of God still eludes our outstretched hopes, his features are not yet clear enough. There is still more in the promise of his invitation.

But we grow weary. Curiosity is no longer enough, nor vague dreams of vague triumph. This race goes to the passionate, to those whose hearts burn within them, who know that their dreams will be fulfilled only beyond the next step and the step after that, who have the heart to finish what they—with God—have started.

## LET US PRAY

Father, in the end,
the only cure for a weary heart
is a renewing glimpse of your face
and a rebirth of passion.
I do not pray, therefore,
to finish the race
but for the heart
to take the next step,
and the next,
and all that follow.

# 3

We touch the surface of good
but never feed on its perfection.

—HILDEGARD OF BINGEN

We ask too little of life.

We live content with what we can already see and measure, wary of what lies just beneath the surface of our days.

We stand at open gateways into the divine, the eternal and the infinite, the ravishingly perfect, the ultimately satisfying. But we forever hesitate, hold back, not trusting all the signs and symbols of welcome, satisfied with the view through cracks in the wall, lured by glimpses of our Father's mansion, spooked by rumors of ghosts and ogres, of guard dogs and dungeons, too spoiled or too afraid to accept our Father at his word: "You are welcome here. This is your home."

Enter now.

## LET US PRAY

If I go to bed tonight,
my soul still lonely,
it is, Father,
by my own choice.
Your invitation is present in every moment,
your nourishing love
just below the surface
of every good thing in my life,
and every bad.

# 4

We breathe the appetizing aroma of food,
but never let it reach our lips
or fill our bellies.

—HILDEGARD OF BINGEN

We are children with our noses against the bakery window. Even though the door stands wide open and the baker is beckoning, we stay where we are, dissuaded by our lack of passion, our petty fears of the unknown, our preference for who we are, our fear of who we might become.

We tease and tempt our souls with passing thoughts of God, with ocean-edge, sunset glimpses of what might be and then walk away convinced that warm feelings are enough, that the scent of food can satisfy our hunger.

We are not yet hungry enough—passionate enough—for God alone.

## LET US PRAY

Let me recognize
that the hunger I feel
is a hunger of my soul
that only you can satisfy.
Let me not dull
that hunger
with a thousand sweet substitutes
for the nourishment
that only you can give.

# 5

We are in danger of withering from apathy, of becoming empty reeds.

—HILDEGARD OF BINGEN

To "wither" is to dry up, to shrivel, to wilt, to lose vigor and freshness, to waste away or decay, to weaken, to languish.

To be "apathetic" is to be without emotion, to lack interest, to be listless, unconcerned, indifferent.

To be an empty reed is to be a skeleton through which life has ceased to flow.

To be without passion is to be all of the above, is to embrace death while we are still alive, is to stand between the abyss and the mountaintop wavering, unsettled and uncommitted, neither sinner nor saint.

No one can come to God, or even to themselves, with only half a heart.

## LET US PRAY

Take this wavering heart
and bring it to new life.
Fill this empty reed
with the breath of your spirit.
And let passion replace
indifference and caution.
Make whole my heart.

# Resurrection

EVELYN UNDERHILL

$B$ecause I have glimpsed
the sparkle of his mysterious radiance
and heard the whisper of his inexorable
demands—
I trust and go on trusting,
in spite of all disconcerting appearances,
my best and deepest longings.
I expect the fulfillment of that sacramental
promise
which is present in all beauty;
the perfect life of the age, the world,
that keeps on drawing near.
I look past process and change,
with all their difficulties and obscurities,
to that perfection which haunts me
because I know that God is perfect,
and his supernatural purpose
must prevail.

—EVELYN UNDERHILL

# Hope

Trust is one of the first things we are taught and one of the last things we learn.

We are taught to trust our parents, and then they and the world, as often as not, tell us that we should be wary of trusting anyone or anything.

We mark our maturity by redefining trust as the badge of a weakling, someone who is dependent, someone who has not yet learned the ways of the world and the basic nasty truths of its streets.

The "trusting soul" is more to be pitied than emulated.

Then we get a glimpse of God and we have to start all over again. We have to unlearn the lessons that life has pounded into our consciousness. The things we most wanted to learn to insure our own survival, the lesson for whose wisdom we have paid the highest price, is precisely the value that we must rid our souls of.

Trust must be reborn as hope.

Our cultivated thick skin must be peeled away to leave our souls open to God and the promises he holds out, the vision in which he invites us to place our trust and embody our hope.

We learn again to trust our "best and deepest longings . . . in spite of all disconcerting appearances."

We look again "past process and change, with all their difficulties and obscurities, to that perfection which haunts us because we know that God is perfect, and his supernatural purpose must prevail."

Our hope is rooted and nourished by that "haunt-ing vision," that once-caught glimpse of what might be, of what, we are confident, truly is.

We learn at last the hardest lesson of all and hope flowers in our souls.

# Evelyn Underhill
## (1875-1941)

She spent her last days in a land where the skies were nightly darkened by bombers and whose familiar streets were paths through what must have seemed like final, unrebuildable ruins.

Winston Churchill's brave words not withstanding, hope must have come hard, even to this remarkably hopeful woman, and to survive the nights her hope must have had roots as deep as she had written about for so many years.

But if the haunting perfection of God and his "supernatural purpose" mean anything at all it is the hope they nourish on the darkest of days. And she had been sharing this hope and preparing for these nights for most of her adult life.

Evelyn Underhill had been a novelist and a poet long before she became one of the most penetrating and popular spiritual writers of the twentieth century. She had worked her spiritual way through the worlds of the occult and magic. She had been enthusiastic about the Hindu poet Tagore and brought to her work her deep, continued interest in contemporaries like

Bergson, Dean Inge, and especially Friedrich von Hugel.

It was a rich mixture held together by her profound grasp of psychological truth common to all the world's religions and her ever-growing commitment to the ordinary, sustaining liturgical and personal prayer life of her beloved Anglican community.

And it was a mixture to which she brought a deep personal prayer life and a skill with language that allowed her to write of the most profound aspects of mysticism in words that made it accessible to all and intimidating to none. As a result almost all of her spiritual books are still in print, new editions abound, and works are just becoming available years after being written.

Her words, like her life, have captured "the sparkle of his mysterious radiance and the whisper of his inexorable demands."

# I

I expect resurrection.

—EVELYN UNDERHILL

Our hope, it seems, always carries with it a hint of doubt. We want something to happen, but maybe it won't.

There's no such wavering for Evelyn Underhill when she talks not just of the future but of every passing moment.

"I expect," she says, "the resurrection." And she means from every death, however little, however frequent.

We have every right to expect the same thing and no need to undermine our hope with "maybes," no need to limit our expectations to possibilities.

There is no final death because "beyond every death is life." Beyond every death is resurrection.

This is not one hope among many but the very heart, the very being of hope itself and therefore of our lives in and with God.

## LET US PRAY

Let me go into this night
willing to die to
all that I have clung to
through this day,
all that I have placed my hope in,
everything in which I have sought life,
through which I have hoped
to find new life.

I can let go, I can surrender.
I can die to this day
because I expect the resurrection of a new day,
of a new life.

# 2

Those who relax their clutch
on what we absurdly call "the" world . . .
do receive a thousandfold.

—EVELYN UNDERHILL

There are moments, let us be honest, when we expect the promised thousandfold of our hope to be paid in the currency of this world.

But hope is its own reward, returning to those who have hope a life that cannot be drowned in discouragement and despair.

For the hope we talk of is not a passing emotion, a rootless yearning for what might be or for what cannot be.

Our hope is in a promise heard, a promise trusted. It is God saying: "You have my word on it."

"I have come that you might have life and have it more abundantly."

It is a fundamental ray of dependability in a world full of promises made solely for a moment's advantage, denied and forgotten when they—we—are no longer needed.

God does not need us. But he never breaks his promises.

## LET US PRAY

I cling to the world
as though there is nothing else,
as though all my hope
is in what I can capture with my eyes,
and clutch in my hands,
like a child with a cookie jar.
But for all the hope I place
in having more,
I end up with less
unless I let go
of everything but you.

# 3

The creative life of God is always coming,
always entering
to refresh and enhance our lives.

—EVELYN UNDERHILL

God never says: "Enough."

He never says: "Your timing is bad. . . . I'm rather tired. . . . Come back when I am not so busy with other more important things, other more important people. . . . I've moved on!"

Above all God never dismisses us as "hopeless cases," unworthy of further attention.

He is "always coming, always entering to refresh and enhance our lives." He is always with us giving hope, sustaining hope, building on our hope. No one is more important. No one has greater claim on his gifts than we.

But we must make room for hope. We must keep the entryway open. It cannot find its way into souls determined to give up, determined to insist that life is too much, that no one cares. Not even God.

The creative life of God, the source of hope, is not there just for the asking. It is ours just for the accepting.

## LET US PRAY

You are always coming,
always entering my heart and soul.
You are always approaching
to refresh and enhance my life.
I need give you
only the slightest opening
and you take advantage of it.
You are my hope,
not there just for the asking,
but mine just for the accepting.
Hear my prayer.
Hear the hope
that gives it life.

# 4

That world which haunts our best moments of prayer and communion will be satisfied.

—EVELYN UNDERHILL

We stop for a quiet moment to set aside the duties and apprehensions of an ordinary day. We pray as best we can. And for that moment the day's noises are muffled and the walls of our lives recede.

We glimpse a world and a life that captures our deepest hope.

When it ends we are tempted to dismiss it as a daydream, as a harmless gossamer fancy, good for a moment's indulgence, but not the stuff of reality, nothing to build a life on. "It's time to go back to the real world."

But there is nothing daydreamish about this moment, this vision.

These haunting visions of a full life are real. They will come true. You can count on it. You can put your hope in them. You will not be disappointed.

Why? Because God, who fashioned your dream, is the guarantor of your hope.

## LET US PRAY

Even as I struggle to find the right words
to bring to you at the end of this day,
I glimpse beyond them a life
beyond my comprehension.

My God, you haunt my words
and fashion all my dreams.
You are not a fantasy.
You are my reality.
Hear my wordless prayer.
Guarantee my hope.

# 5

The note we end on is and must be
the note of inexhaustible possibility and hope.

—EVELYN UNDERHILL

When she wrote of the "end," Evelyn Underhill was referring to the final chapter of a book and to the final vision of the Apostle's Creed.

But she could have meant the "end" of our lives, and the "end" of this and every day. For the final step of our spiritual journey and the last moments of this day will be like the first and all the steps that have followed. It will be taken in hope.

So we let go of this dying day. But we do not go hopelessly into the dark. Even as we surrender the security of what we have come to know it is for the sake of awakening to and embracing an unknown and unknowable new day where God will keep his promises.

We will go there with nothing to cling to but the word of God in whom we believe, in whose presence and in whose words we place our trust.

This hope of ours is the bridge between today and tomorrow, between what we know and the unknowable. And it is enough.

## LET US PRAY

I let go of this dying day.
But I do not go hopelessly into the dark,
but with a soul filled
with inexhaustible possibility and hope.
For even as I surrender the security
of what I have come to know
and rely on,
I hear your promise of a new day,
and the knowledge that I will awake
to the unknown and unknowable,
to that place where
you will keep your promises.

# PART THREE

# God Present

The Lord is my shepherd, I shall not want;
I lie down in green pastures.
God leads me beside restful waters,
restoring my soul.
I walk the way of truth
for the sake of God's name.
Even though I walk through
the valley of the shadow of death,
I fear no evil,
for you are with me.
Your rod and your staff give me comfort.
You set a table before me
in the presence of my enemies,
you anoint my head with oil,
and my cup overflows.

—THE PSALMIST

If our hunger for God is, as we might have feared or as others might have judged, madness or at best foolishness, we now know that we are not alone.

We are in very good company.

Generations of mystics have known what it is like to be God hungry. They have been where we find ourselves, they have done what we seek to do. They know far better than we why our souls ache.

They have volunteered to be our companions on the way, which is a good thing. For the road on which we have set foot is a treacherous one. Mad men and fools have indeed traveled it and still do. There are false guides, spiritual "hustlers" at every intersection offering safer paths, more exotic, trendier ones. They are eager to point out popular, more understandable destinations. "Why do you insist on being different? . . . You're in over your head. . . . I'll show you a shortcut. . . . Tell you what I'm going to do."

It's hard not to pay attention to those offering bargain rates and shortcuts. On any given day any other road can seem preferable to the one we have chosen. But chances are that we have tried those roads and come up empty, lost, unsatisfied with where they have led us.

Our hunger is for God and only God can satisfy it. Our path is the path of the mystics.

We are not mad. We are not fools. Nor are we dreamers of impossible dreams.

We have caught a glimpse of what the mystics saw.

Studying their lives, reading their words has made us even more discontented with shallow trivializing of our lives and dreams, with so much of what today passes for "spirituality." Tasting the real thing has intensified our spiritual appetite for a life beyond greeting card wisdom, beyond this season's ten rules for this and seven steps to that. We are losing our taste for whatever psycho-babble is masquerading this year as wisdom.

Walking in the company of the mystics, we are now less likely to confuse spirituality with warm-fuzziness. We are in less danger of mistaking garden paths for the hard, obstacle-strewn, always, it seems, steeply-upward road of faith.

Praying with them, we are overcoming our dependence on the right words, the right time, the right place, or the right mood. Above all we have come to know and accept that there is no guarantee of hearing God's reply, or even of experiencing a sense that we have been heard.

True, in the company of the mystics our journey seems a little easier. We hear them say: "You think you're having it hard, let me tell you! . . . Here, take my hand. . . . I've been here before. . . . Just keep walking. . . . You can't imagine what lies ahead. . . . You can't imagine what's in store for you!"

We know, moreover, that in such hands we are in less danger of falling victim to false visions of spiritual grandeur. The mystics are the realists of spirituality. They know all about living lives of blind faith, of dark days and nights, when God hides his face and the soul cries out for just one moment of warmth, of reassurance.

It is important, however, to understand that despite their companionship, we will not be excused from writing new chapters in the history of prayer.

The invitation to "come follow me" may always be the same but it is never delivered twice in the same way, certainly never in the same context. For no two people can hear it in the same way, no two people will respond in the same way. Our names are not Teresa of Avila or John of the Cross, and the time in which we live and the personal history we carry with us make their own special demands and offer their own special opportunities. No one has ever before heard the invitation in exactly the same way it has come to us.

Our moment is unique even though we have chosen not to walk alone.

The mystics' words may soar within us and fuel our imaginations. We may share their soul-stretching, almost embarrassing dreams, but their stories are achingly familiar, encouragingly human, filled with familiar, common, recognizable pain and frustration. We are in the company of real human beings who like us set out, perhaps cautiously, perhaps wildly, on a spiritual journey believing that they have heard God's voice in their ears and felt his breath on their souls.

Choosing to walk with them means choosing more than balm for our aches and placebos for our souls. We leave behind our desire to tranquilize our most daring dreams, our desire to seek out God "this week only at bargain prices." And we choose to ignore the thousand other volunteers so willing to provide advice and encouragement to stop our search short of God, the thousand voices who tell us: "That's enough, don't strain yourself."

With the mystics as our companions we choose to pay full price, to hear the truth and desire more than anything else to live it. We have believable guides, friends to be enjoyed, teachers to be trusted.

With all this inspiration, however, and encouragement, for all their truth telling, we still have to walk the walk and pray the prayer. They can't do it for us. The most profound truth, however, is that neither can we do it for ourselves. And we needn't. Only God can do what only God can do.

Only God can satisfy our hunger. The mystics are with us to remind us of this fundamental truth, not to substitute for our surrender, but to hold our hands and reaffirm our dreams.

*They will keep us focused.*

At every intersection of our lives there will be no shortage of honorable, valid, interesting, and inviting directions to take and good reasons for taking any one of them.

Their attraction will not be something evil, just another possibility competing for our attention, something closer to hand, something more available, something that in the heat of the day blinds us to what we have seen at the end of the road we have chosen.

There will be many such moments and turnings, but we can't take every path or follow every rainbow. And we may have to bypass a sunny, quiet, wooded path for a treacherous, badly lighted, scary city, noisy with demands.

It will not be easy staying focused, putting all our energy at the service of our dreams. But keeping our end clearly, unwaveringly in sight is a condition of any successful journey.

*They will keep us honest.*

When the soul glimpses a world of great, even dramatic spirituality, it is very easy to lose sight of the basics—things like honesty.

Honesty is about reality. And reality can slip away in quiet moments spent in the company of visionary mystics—where the mansions of the spirit are a more inviting and comfortable residence than the everyday world where true spirituality is always rooted.

In those moments we can easily convince ourselves that what we want to be true is already true.

Mistaking the first step for the whole journey we may find ourselves overlooking painful truths about our lives that will have to be confronted if we are to take even a second step.

*They will keep us humble.*

Nothing scuttles the spiritual journey more thoroughly than pride, the insidious feeling that we are not like the others—sinners. We are mystics in the making. We walk with saints. See how we pray!

But if we listen to our companions on the way we will hear them say very clearly: "Get over it. The time has not come—it never will—for parading your virtues."

It is the insistence of their voices and our openness to their words that make them far more reliable companions for the journey than family and friends too willing to cheer our smallest efforts—certainly far more reliable than our egos starved for praise.

"Trust us," they say. "You have a long way to go. But you are not alone."

*They will keep us at it.*

The first step may be a long time coming. But it can also be the easiest.

What counts is our willingness to go on walking when our souls ache and the vision that once fired our dreams is dim and hidden from us behind walls of weariness.

We need someone at our side who knows from experience what lies one step beyond where we are, and one more step beyond that, and one more, and a thousand more.

We will need their encouragement when after those thousand steps it will seem that we have not moved at all. We will need someone who can say to us, "Keep walking, keep at it, you won't regret a step of the way."

*They will keep us from settling for too little when we have been offered so much.*

Spirituality is about achieving a profound self-esteem, that is, coming to see ourselves as God sees us, the object of infinite love, unremitting solicitude, the bearers of God's greatest dreams for humanity.

The temptation is to think they are talking about others. We are lucky and happy just to get by.

It may sound like suitable modesty.

But it can in fact be a way of taking ourselves off the spiritual hook, our way of settling for very little, for choosing to go home hungry from the banquet that has been set before us. However, with the mystics at our side calling our bluff, keeping us honest, reminding us that we have been invited to the feast, we are less likely to go away hungry.

We need them to remind and reassure us that it is okay to dream of the spiritual best. It is after all not a question of our qualifications but only of our willingness to let God have his way with us.

◆ ◆ ◆

This book has been about spending time with all the right people.

The mystics have taken us across denominational and religious lines because in the purity of their vision those distinctions mean almost nothing to them. They have sought and found God, and everything else has seemed to them to be very small change.

They have not offered us spiritual junk food or denominational propaganda. They have watered down nothing.

We began our journey knowing that it is the experience of God we seek, and the mystics have made sure that the time we have spent with them has not been wasted along side roads or promising but circular paths that lead back to our own poverty.

This book, hopefully, has been for you more than a travelogue, more than an armchair journey into the heart of God and your own soul, more too than a practice run. By praying this book and not just reading it, you have taken real steps along the way.

In the presence of the mystics, in their stories, we can know with certitude the most important thing of all: it can be done. We can find God. We can live in God's presence. We already do.

For we eat at his table. Our cup overflows.